Contents

LEARNING TO USE MY BIBLE

STUDENT GUIDE

EDITORIAL / DESIGN TEAM

Laura Allison ....Editor/Writer
Heidi Hewitt ....Production Editor
Jim Carlton...Designer

Cover Design: Jim Carlton
Cover Art & Photos: Shutterstock

Art Credits: Shutterstock, Brenda Gilliam (pp. 2, 20, 29), Diana Magnuson (p. 4), Megan Jeffery (p. 9)

LEARNING TO USE MY BIBLE: STUDENT GUIDE: An official resource for The United Methodist Church approved by Discipleship Ministries and published by Abingdon Press, a division of The United Methodist Publishing House, 2222 Rosa L. Parks Blvd., Nashville, TN 37228-1306. Price $7.99. Copyright © 2019 Abingdon Press. All rights reserved. Printed in the United States of America.

To order copies of this publication, call toll free: **800-672-1789**. You may fax your order to 800-445-8189. Telecommunication Device for the Deaf/Telex Telephone: 800-227-4091. Or order online at **cokesbury.com**. Use your Cokesbury account, American Express, Visa, Discover, or Mastercard.

For information concerning permission to reproduce any material in this publication, write to Rights and Permissions, The United Methodist Publishing House, 2222 Rosa L. Parks Blvd., Nashville, TN 37228-1306. You may fax your request to 615-749-6128. Or e-mail *permissions@umpublishing.org*.

If you have questions or comments, call toll free: **800-672-1789**. Or e-mail **customerhelp@cokesbury.com**.

19 20 21 22 23 24 25 26 27 28—10 9 8 7 6 5 4 3 2 1
PACP10544754-01

Abingdon Press

Color-Coded Bookmark

Use a Color-Coded Bookmark to mark your Bible.

1. Use the black yarn of your bookmark to mark the Contents page in your Bible.

2. Use the green yarn to mark Genesis, the first book of Law in your Bible.

3. Use the teal yarn to mark Joshua, the first Old Testament book of History in your Bible.

4. Use the light blue yarn to mark Psalms, the second book of Poetry in your Bible.

5. Use the dark blue yarn to mark Isaiah, the first book of Prophets in your Bible.

6. Use the yellow yarn to mark Matthew, the first Gospel book in your Bible.

7. Use the dark red yarn to mark Romans, the first book of Letters in your Bible.

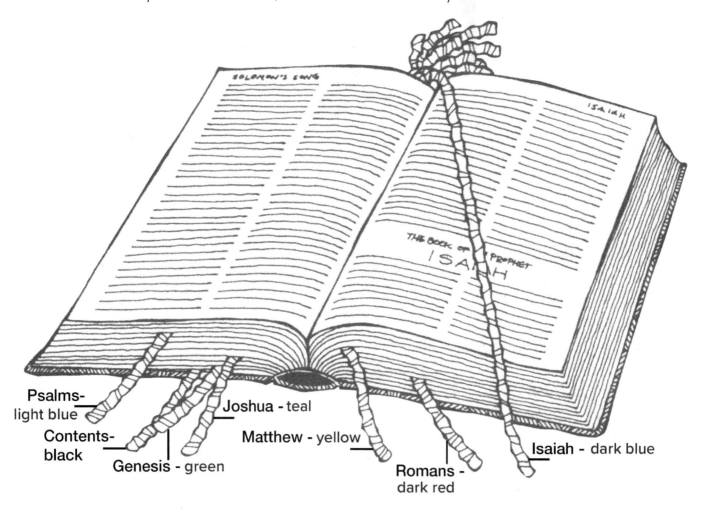

Psalms- light blue

Contents- black

Genesis - green

Joshua - teal

Matthew - yellow

Romans - dark red

Isaiah - dark blue

A Book Like No Other

Use the cryptogram to crack the code and discover some important facts about the Bible.

A	B	C	D	E	F	G	H	I	J	K	L	M	N	O	P	Q	R	S	T	U	V	W	X	Y	Z
L	M	N	O	P	Q	R	S	T	U	V	W	X	Y	Z	A	B	C	D	E	F	G	H	I	J	K

0	1	2	3	4	5	6	7	8	9
9	7	5	6	1	8	3	4	2	0

The Bible is a ___ ___ ___ ___ ___ ___ ___ with ___ ___ books.
A X Q G P G N   3 3

The Bible is divided into two main sections: ___ ___ ___ Testament and ___ ___ ___ Testament.
D A S   C T L

The Old Testament has ___ ___ books and tells about the ___ ___ ___ ___ ___ ___ of
6 0   W X H I D G N

the ___ ___ ___ ___ ___ ___ ___ ___ ___ .
X H G P T A X I T H

The New Testament has ___ ___ books and tells about the ___ ___ ___ ___ ___ ___ ___ ___ ___ ___
8 1   A X U T   D U   Y T H J H

and the ___ ___ ___ ___ ___ ___ .
R W J G R W

The Old Testament was written over a period of ___ , ___ ___ ___ years.
4 9 9 9

The original copies of the Bible were written in ___ languages: ___ ___ ___ ___ ___ ___ , Aramaic,
6   W T Q G T L

and ___ ___ ___ ___ ___ .
V G T T Z

The Bible also is called the ___ ___ ___ ___ ___ ___ ___ ___ ___ , the Holy Bible, the Scriptures, and some
L D G S   D U   V D S

people call it a ___ ___ ___ ___ ___ ___ ___ ___ ___ ___ ___ .
V X U I   U G D B   V D S

Psalm 119:105

Your word is a lamp before my feet and a light for my journey.

Your (God's)

Point with your right hand, then raise the palm of your right hand to the sky. Bring the hand down in front of your face, as if you are drawing a shepherd's crook. Open the palm as you bring your hand down. End with your palm facing left.

Word

Hold the first finger of your left hand in front of you. Touch that finger twice with the first finger and thumb of your right hand.

Light / Lamp

With fingertips touching, move your right hand up beside your head and spread your fingers apart.

Feet

Hold your left hand out with your palm facing down. With the first finger of your right hand, point by the left side of your left hand and then by the right side.

Journey (Travel)

Hold the first and middle fingers of your right hand up and slightly curved. Touch your thumb to the other two fingers. Make three small circles clockwise.

Events in the Books of Law

Choose the best description for the focus of each book of Law. Write each number in the circle with the name of the book. If you need help, read the introduction for each book in the *Deep Blue Kids Bible*.

1. Contains instructions for the tribe of Levi to establish the priesthood and to serve as spiritual leaders

2. Contains the stories of Creation, Noah and the Flood, and the beginnings of God's people (the Israelites)

3. Describes how Moses counted the Israelites as they prepared to enter the Promised Land

4. Contains Moses' speeches about the important things the Israelites needed to know to move into the Promised Land

5. Tells about God delivering the Israelites from slavery in Egypt and beginning their journey to the Promised Land

Genesis

Deuteronomy

Exodus

Books of Law, Torah, Pentateuch

Numbers

Leviticus

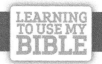

Patriarchs' Family Tree

God told Abraham that his descendants would be too many to count, like the stars in the sky. Abraham's grandson Jacob (later named Israel) had 12 sons who became the tribes of Israel. They received a territory when the Israelites entered the Promised Land. Read Genesis 35:23-26 to find the names of the 12 sons. The tribe of Levi, the Levites, became the priests and didn't receive any territory. They served all of the tribes. Joseph's territory was divided into 2 sections and given to his sons, Ephraim and Manasseh. Fill in Abraham's family tree. Start with Abraham and Sarah. Read Genesis 25:19-26 if you need help. Highlight the names of the 12 people whose tribes were given territory in the Promised Land.

Patriarchs' Family Tree

Make a Bible Library Bookmark

Color your bookmark. Cut it out and punch a hole in the top. Thread a piece of ribbon through the hole, and tie the ends together.

Note to the Leader: Photocopy this page on card stock for each student to color and cut out.

Bible Library

OLD TESTAMENT

Law
Genesis
Exodus
Leviticus
Numbers
Deuteronomy

History
Joshua
Judges
Ruth
1 Samuel
2 Samuel
1 Kings
2 Kings
1 Chronicles
2 Chronicles
Ezra
Nehemiah
Esther

Poetry
Job
Psalms
Proverbs

Ecclesiastes
Song of Songs

Major Prophets
Isaiah
Jeremiah
Lamentations
Ezekiel
Daniel

Minor Prophets
Hosea
Joel
Amos
Obadiah
Jonah
Micah
Nahum
Habakkuk
Zephaniah
Haggai
Zechariah
Malachi

NEW TESTAMENT

Gospels
Matthew
Mark
Luke
John

History
Acts

Paul's Letters
Romans
1 Corinthians
2 Corinthians
Galatians
Ephesians
Philippians
Colossians
1 Thessalonians
2 Thessalonians

1 Timothy
2 Timothy
Titus
Philemon

General Letters
Hebrews
James
1 Peter
2 Peter
1 John
2 John
3 John
Jude

Prophecy
Revelation

deepbluekids@cokesbury.com **7**

The Law

After the Israelites left Egypt, they became a large traveling community led by Moses. God spoke to Moses when he was leading the Israelites through the wilderness. God gave him laws for the Israelites to live by. Read these 2 passages of laws. What do they mean to you? Rewrite them in your own words.

The Ten Commandments (Exodus 20:1-17)

1. You must have no other gods before me.
_____
_____

2. Do not make an idol for yourself... Do not bow down to them or worship them.
_____
_____

3. Do not use the LORD your God's name as if it were of no significance.
_____
_____

4. Remember the Sabbath day and treat it as holy.
_____
_____

5. Honor your father and your mother.
_____

6. Do not kill.
_____

7. Do not commit adultery.
_____

8. Do not steal.
_____

9. Do not testify falsely against your neighbor.
_____
_____

10. Do not desire...anything... that belongs to your neighbor.
_____
_____

Shema (Deuteronomy 6:5-9)

Love the LORD your God with all your heart, all your being, and all your strength. These words that I am commanding you today must always be on your minds. Recite them to your children. Talk about them when you are sitting around your house and when you are out and about, when you are lying down and when you are getting up. Tie them on your hand as a sign. They should be on your forehead as a symbol. Write them on your house's doorframes and on your city's gates.

_____
_____

Promised Land Maze

Put the number 1 in the Start box and 12 in the End box. Number the other boxes as you make your way through the maze and discover what happened to the Israelites in the Promised Land.

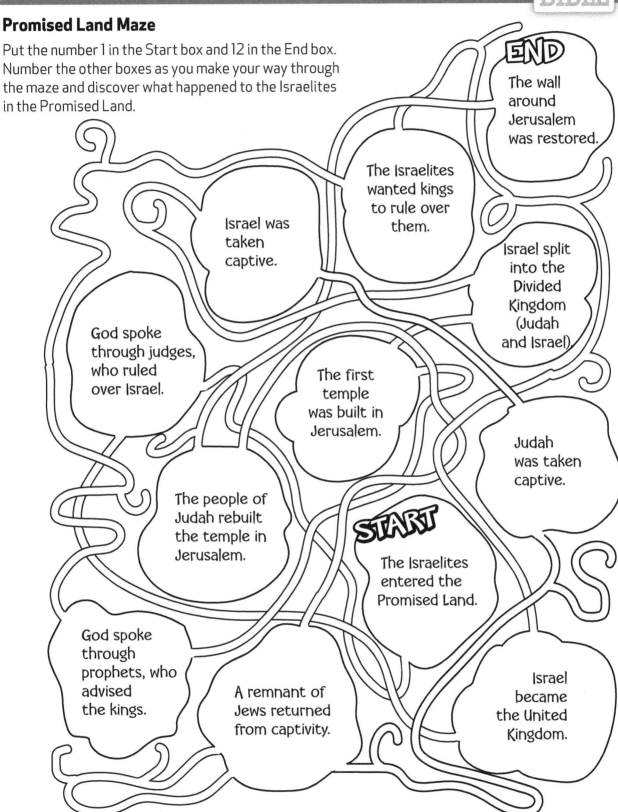

Guess Who

Match the person's name with the description of that person. First, fill in the answers you know. Then, use the *Deep Blue Kids Bible Dictionary* to help you find the other answers.

Nehemiah
Deborah
Saul
Joshua
Elisha
Gideon
Esther
David
Samson
Elijah
Ruth
Samuel
Ezra
Solomon

1._____
I was Moses' assistant in the wilderness.
I became the leader of the Israelites and led them into the Promised Land.
I led the march around Jericho.

5._____
I followed my mother-in-law and worshipped her God.
I am an ancestor of David and Jesus.

9._____
I was raised by a priest.
I was a prophet and the last judge of Israel.
I anointed the first 2 kings of Israel.

2._____
I was a prophetess.
I was the only woman judge of Israel.

6._____
I was the first king of Israel.
I loved and hated David.

10._____
I was a prophet.
I was taken to heaven on a chariot in a windstorm.

3._____
I was a judge of Israel.
I asked God to give me a sign to show God's will.

7._____
I was a shepherd.
I played the harp.
I was known as a great king of Israel.

11._____
I was a prophet.
I was trained by Elijah.

13._____
I was a cupbearer for the king of Persia during the time of the exile.
After the Jews returned from Babylon, I supervised the rebuilding of the walls of Jerusalem.

4._____
I was a judge.
I was famous for my long hair.
I lost my strength when my hair was cut.

8._____
I was king of Israel.
I built the temple in Jerusalem.
I am famous for my great wisdom.

12._____
I was a priest during the time the Jews were in exile.
I was sent back to Jerusalem when the Jews began to return.
I helped the Israelites restore the temple.

14._____
I was a Jewish orphan and lived with my cousin.
I became the queen of Persia.
I helped save the Jews from death.

deepbluekids@cokesbury.com

BIBLE PASSAGES ACTIVITY / 3C

Find / Change

The Scriptures below are familiar passages. But there's a problem; they have mistakes in them. Find the passages in your Bible. Cross through the mistakes and write those words correctly on the lines.

Joshua 1:9b

Don't be happy or sad,

_____

because the LORD your God is with you at church.

_____

Ruth 1:16b, c

Wherever you go, I might go;

_____

and wherever you stay, I won't stay.

_____

Your people may be my people,

_____

but your God will not be my God.

_____

1 Samuel 16:7b, c

God doesn't look at things like humans do. Humans see into the heart, but the LORD

_____

sees only what is visible to the eyes.

_____

2 Kings 22:2a

He did what was right in his own eyes.

_____

Esther 4:14c

Maybe it was for a minute like this that

_____

you came to live with Mordecai's family.

_____

Proverbs 17:17

Friends love when they like what you do,

_____

and kinsfolk probably won't help you in times of trouble.

_____

Psalm 23:1-3

The LORD is my shepherd.
   I need so much.

_____

He won't let me rest anywhere;

_____

   he leads me to rapid-flowing waters;

_____

   he makes me unhappy.

_____

He guides me to rough paths

_____

   for the sake of making me work hard.

_____

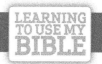
Psalm 105:1-5

Give thanks to the LORD; call upon his name; make his deeds known to all people!

Thank you, God, for all your wonderful works.

Sing to God; sing praises to the LORD; dwell on all his wondrous works!

I will praise you by singing about your wonderful works.

Give praise to God's holy name! Let the hearts rejoice of all those seeking the LORD!

My heart rejoices when I praise your holy name.

Pursue the LORD and his strength; seek his face always!

I will follow you, LORD, and seek your face.

Remember the wondrous works he has done, all his marvelous works, and the justice he declared.

Thank you, God, for all your wonderful works.

Psalm 105:1-5

I Witness News Report

News Announcer: This is *(name)* with I Witness News. We have breaking news. Some of the people we read about in the Old Testament have gathered in Jerusalem. Our I Witness News reporter is at the scene. Let's go live to the scene to our reporter, *(name)*.

Reporter: Thank you, *(name)*. This is an amazing scene! Bible characters who lived before Jesus was born are gathered at the temple site in Jerusalem. They have a story to tell, and we are going to interview them live. Let's start with Adam and Eve, the first humans. Adam and Eve, can you tell us about your time in the garden?

Adam: Thank you for asking. God created the earth and everything in it for us. God let me name all the animals, and God created Eve.

Eve: The garden was so beautiful. We had everything we needed. God said our job was to take care of God's creation. We enjoyed that very much. God gave us only 1 rule: Don't eat the fruit from the tree of knowledge of good and evil. The garden was full of fruit trees, but we broke God's rule. We had to leave the garden, but God provided for us. He loved us even though we had disobeyed him.

Reporter: Thank you, Adam and Eve. Let's talk to Noah now. Noah, how did you get all those animals in the ark?

Noah: The ark was definitely full, but we made it. God gave me specific directions to follow to build the ark and what animals to take in the ark. I did exactly what God said, even though a lot of my neighbors said I was crazy. We were in the ark a long time. The waters finally went down, and God sent a beautiful rainbow as a promise that we wouldn't have to go through a flood like that again.

Reporter: Thank you, Noah. I see Abraham coming toward me. I believe God gave him a special promise, too.

Abraham: Yes, God promised me I would have so many descendants that I wouldn't be able to count them. Sarah and I were really old, so we struggled to believe God's promise. But God did exactly what God promised and sent us a son named Isaac, which, by the way, means "laughter." Isaac had a son named Jacob, who had 12 sons. God used my great-grandchildren to form the tribes of Israel and gave them territory in the Promised Land.

Reporter: It's great getting to talk to all of you. Let's see how many more people I can interview. I'll go down the line, and you can tell us the most important thing that happened to you.

Joseph: My brothers sold me as a slave, but years later the pharaoh in Egypt made me his second-in-command. God allowed me to help save my family from a great famine.

Moses: It's hard to choose the most important event from my life, but I think it was the day God spoke to me from a burning bush. God sent me to free my people who were slaves in Egypt. Leading the Israelites through the wilderness to the Promised Land was a wonderful adventure.

Joshua: Moses made me the leader of the Israelites, and I'm so thankful for everything he taught me. God gave us instructions and told us that God would be with us always. So, we entered the Promised Land, and we split the territory between all the tribes.

Samuel: God continued giving us instructions. Judges ruled over Israel, and God spoke to the people through them. I was the last judge. The people wanted a king like all the other nations, so I anointed the first 2 kings, Saul and David. Solomon, David's son, was the third king, and he led the people to build a temple for worship in Jerusalem. These kings ruled over a united kingdom, and God spoke to the people through prophets. But Israel didn't stay united. Problems arose, and the country divided into Israel and Judah. Eventually, both countries were defeated and taken captive to foreign lands.

Daniel: When Babylon defeated us, my friends and I were taken captive and chosen to serve the king. We kept worshipping our God the way we were taught. My friends were thrown into a fiery furnace because they wouldn't worship an idol, and I was thrown in the lions' pit because I wouldn't stop praying to God. But God saved all 4 of us, and we continued worshipping God.

Ezra: Eventually, we were released from captivity and returned to Jerusalem. God gave me instructions to lead the people to restore the temple.

Malachi: God gave me a message for the people: Love God and love one another. You have hope in God.

Reporter: Thank you all for your stories! God did amazing things in your time, and God's story is still continuing today.

Match the Prophets with the Words

The chapter and verse are given after each Scripture. Decide which of the 4 prophets wrote the words in his book, then write his name on the blank line above the verse.

1. _____

God's name be praised from age to eternal age! Wisdom and might are his! (2:20)

2. _____

A child is born to us, a son is given to us, and authority will be on his shoulders. He will be named Wonderful Counselor, Mighty God, Eternal Father, Prince of Peace. (9:6)

3. _____

I called out to the LORD in my distress, and he answered me. From the belly of the underworld I cried out for help; you have heard my voice. (2:2)

4. _____

The LORD God's spirit is upon me, because the LORD has anointed me. He has sent me to bring good news to the poor, to bind up the brokenhearted, to proclaim release for captives. (61:1)

5. _____

I know the plans I have in mind for you, declares the LORD; they are plans for peace, not disaster, to give you a future filled with hope. When you call me and come and pray to me, I will listen to you. When you search for me, yes, search for me with all your heart, you will find me. (29:11-13)

6. _____

My God sent his messenger, who shut the lions' mouths. They haven't touched me because I was judged innocent before my God. (6:22)

7. _____

I will give them a heart to know me, for I am the LORD. They will be my people, and I will be their God, for they will return to me with all their heart. (24:7)

8. _____

I know that you are a merciful and compassionate God, very patient, full of faithful love, and willing not to destroy. (4:2d)

BIBLE PASSAGES ACTIVITY / 4C

Discover the Prophets' Words

Use the code to fill in the missing letters, and you will discover some words of wisdom from the minor prophets.

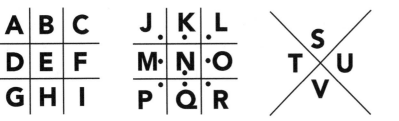

Let _ _ _ _ _ _ _ roll down like _ _ _ _ _ _. (_ _ _ _ 5:24)

He has told you…what is _ _ _ _ and what the _ _ _ _ requires from you. (_ _ _ _ _ 6:8)

The LORD is good, a _ _ _ _ _ _ in a day of _ _ _ _ _ _ _ _. (_ _ _ _ _ 1:7)

Show _ _ _ _ _ _ _ _ and _ _ _ _ _ _ _ _ _ _ to each other! (_ _ _ _ _ _ _ _ _ 7:9)

BONUS

Read Joel 2:28. What did the prophet say would be given to everyone? When did this prophecy come true?

_____   _____

Prayer Station

God spoke through the prophets to the Israelites. The prophets would pray and ask for God's guidance. Then they would tell the people what God told them.

The Holy Spirit speaks to us and leads us. With the Spirit's help, God can show us what we need to STOP doing, God can WARN us of who and what to be cautious of, and God often tells us to GO and do things.

Does that remind you of a traffic light? The top color, red, means stop. The middle color, yellow, is a warning to get ready to stop. And the bottom color, green, means go.

You can pray and ask God to show you what you need to stop doing, what you need a warning to be cautious about doing, and what you need to go and do. Color the lights red, yellow, and green, and then write under each traffic light what God puts on your heart.

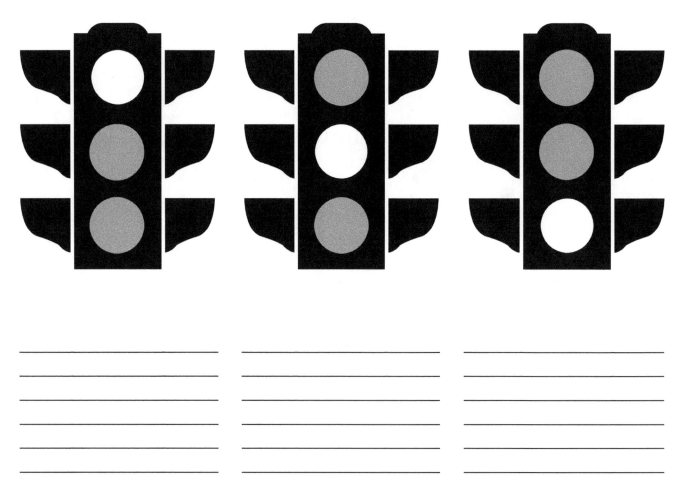

The Gospels

The writers of the 4 Gospels all told about the life of Jesus. Choose 1 of the Gospels to answer the questions in the boxes below.

All About the Book of _____

Is this book in the Old or New Testament?

What division is this book in?

What does the author write about in this book?

Does this Gospel tell about Jesus' birth? If so, what part of the story is included?

How does this writer present Jesus?

Does this Gospel include any parables? If so, write the name of a parable you like.

What is a special Scripture passage you found in this book?

What is your favorite of Jesus' miracles recorded in this book?

What other special events did the author write about?

Jesus Chose the Twelve

Look up Luke 6:13-16 to find the names of the 12 men Jesus picked to be his disciples. Write them on these lines.

_____   _____   _____

_____   _____   _____

_____   _____   _____

_____   _____   _____

Who Am I?

Can you match the disciples' names with their descriptions? Fill in the ones you know, and then try to guess as many of the remaining ones as you can in the time given. If you need help, look in Matthew 9 and 26; Mark 3; 14; and 15; Luke 6; John 1; 6; 18; 19; and 20. You also may find help in the *Deep Blue Kids Bible Dictionary* or in the concordance in the *CEB Study Bible*.

1. I denied knowing Jesus three times on the night he was arrested. _____

2. I betrayed Jesus. _____

3. I introduced my brother to Jesus. _____

4. I am sometimes known as Nathanael. _____

5. I am also called Thaddaeus. _____

6. I was a tax collector before Jesus called me to be his disciple. _____

7. I talked about salary (money) when Jesus asked about food in the story of Jesus feeding the 5,000.

_____

8. I usually have a couple words attached to my first name. _____

9. I am often called "doubting" because I didn't believe in the Resurrection until I had proof.

_____

10. I have the same first name as another disciple, so I sometimes am called "the younger."

_____

11. Before Jesus died on the cross, he asked me to take care of his mother, and I did.

_____

12. I am part of the inner circle of 3 disciples (along with Peter and John) who were closest to Jesus.

_____

BONUS

My name means "gift of God." Who am I? _____

My name means "twin." Who Am I? _____

The People Jesus Met

Draw a line from each event, miracle, or parable to the person involved. For help with matching, look up these scriptures: Matthew 3; Mark 5; Mark 10; Luke 10; Luke 15; Luke 17; Luke 19; John 3; and John 4.

1. I asked my father for my inheritance, and then I left home.

Samaritan woman at the well

2. A Pharisee met Jesus at night to ask Jesus questions.

Jairus

3. Jesus offered me "living water."

Zacchaeus

4. A tax collector who was short climbed a tree.

children

5. I took care of a man lying beside the road who had been beaten.

prodigal son

6. Jesus said God's kingdom belongs to people like this group.

John the Baptist

7. Jesus healed a blind man and made him see.

man with a skin disease

8. I didn't think I was good enough to baptize Jesus.

Nicodemus

9. I was the only 1 out of 10 who thanked Jesus for healing us.

good Samaritan

10. My daughter was dead, but Jesus healed her.

Bartimaeus

BONUS (Look up John 2 for help.)

What was the first miracle Jesus performed? _____

Where was Jesus when he did the miracle? _____

Who asked Jesus to do the miracle? _____

Teachings of Jesus

Not long after Jesus was baptized, he went up on a mountainside and preached a sermon. We sometimes call it the Sermon on the Mount, and it is in Matthew 5–7. Jesus started with the Beatitudes. He told the crowd that they would be happy in their hearts if they lived God's way. Use your Bible to find the missing words and to complete the crossword puzzle.

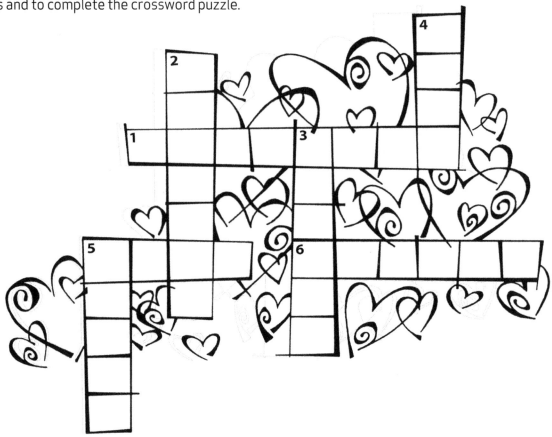

Across

1. Where your _____ is, there your heart will be also. (Matthew 6:21)

5. But I say to you, _____ your enemies and pray for those who harass you. (Matthew 5:44)

6. Give to those who ask, and don't _____ those who wish to borrow from you. (Matthew 5:42)

Down

2. If you _____ others their sins, your heavenly Father will also forgive you. (Matthew 6:14)

3. Ask, and you will receive. _____, and you will find. Knock, and the door will be opened to you. (Matthew 7:7)

4. Everybody who hears these words of mine and puts them into practice is like a _____ builder who built a house on bedrock. (Matthew 7:24)

5. Let your _____ shine before people, so they can see the good things you do and praise your Father who is in heaven. (Matthew 5:16)

deepbluekids@cokesbury.com

The Church Begins: Pentecost

Jesus said, "Don't be troubled or afraid."

(Hold your hands out in front of you, as if you're afraid.)

"God will send the Holy Spirit to be your Companion."

(Lift your hands above your head, then bring them down in front of you.)

Jesus' followers gathered in an upper room in Jerusalem to celebrate the Day of Pentecost.

(Move your arms like you're gathering up something.)

Suddenly, a fierce, howling wind filled the room.

(Sway your arms back and forth.)

Then little flames of fire fell on the followers, but no one was burned.

(Hold your hands in front of you with the palms facing each other. Spread your fingers apart, and wiggle them back and forth.)

They were all filled with the Holy Spirit.

(Place your hands in front of you, and move them from your legs to your head.)

And they spoke in languages they hadn't learned.

(Touch your mouth with your fingers, then move your hands away from your mouth.)

The crowd outside heard the noise.

(Cup your hands over your ears and shake your hands back and forth.)

Peter preached a sermon, and the people heard it in their own languages.

(Cup your hands over your ears.)

The crowd cried out, "What should we do?"

(Touch your mouth with your fingers. Then move your hands quickly away from you.)

Peter told them, "Change your hearts and lives."

(Face your body to the left. Then turn to the right.)

Three thousand people were baptized.

(Hold up your fingers—1, 2, 3—and move the other hand away from the 3 fingers.)

The church began that day.

(Move your arms above your head and bring your fingers together like a steeple.)

The Church Grows: Early Church Leaders

Many people helped the apostles start new churches. Use the words in the word bank to fill in the blanks to discover some of these people. If you need help, use the *Deep Blue Kids Bible Dictionary.*

1. __ __ __ __ __ __ __ __ was one of the 7 men chosen to serve the church of Jerusalem.

2. A Gentile named __ __ __ __ __ opened her home in Philippi for Paul and Silas.

3. __ __ __ __ __ __ __ __ __ and __ __ __ __ __ __ opened their home in Corinth for Paul to meet with the church.

4. __ __ __ __ __ __ __ __ was a leader in the church of Antioch. His name means "one who encourages."

5. Paul asked a young man with a good reputation in the church to accompany him on missionary journeys. His name was __ __ __ __ __ __ __ .

6. __ __ __ __ __ __ __ , a disciple in the city of Joppa, was known for her good works and acts of charity.

7. __ __ __ __ __ traveled with Paul on missionary journeys.

Lydia

Priscilla and Aquila

Stephen   Silas   Barnabas

Tabitha   Timothy

deepbluekids@cokesbury.com

The Church Spreads: Missionary Journeys

A few of the apostles stayed in Jerusalem to take care of the church of Jerusalem. The rest of the apostles traveled to other areas. They helped start churches in Judea, India, Asia, Europe, countries around the Black Sea, and the Mesopotamian region. John was exiled to the island of Patmos, where he wrote to the 7 churches of Asia.

And Paul wrote letters to some of the churches he helped start. These letters became books in our Bible. Draw a line from each book of the Bible to the city where the church was located. Then locate these cities on the "Bible-Times Map" (Class Pack—p. 19).

Romans	Philippi
Corinthians	Thessalonica
Galatians	Rome
Ephesians	Ephesus
Philippians	Corinth
Colossians	Galatia
Thessalonians	Colossae

Acts 1:8

Before Jesus went back to God, he commissioned his apostles as missionaries. With the help of the Holy Spirit, the apostles carried out their mission to spread the good news from their city (Jerusalem), to their countries (Judea and Samaria), and to the world.

In the small circle, write the name of the city where you live. Write 1 way you can help your church in your city.

In the medium circle, write the name of the country where you live. Write 1 way you can help the churches in your country.

In the large circle, write 1 way you can help the churches all over the world.

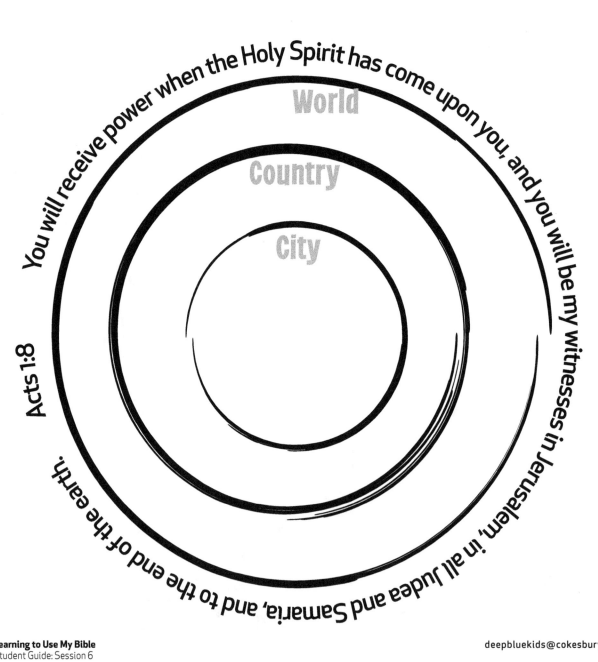

Apostles and Epistles

Group A: Apostles,

Group B: epistles—

All: words that we should know.

Group A: Some apostles

Group B: wrote epistles,

All: helping the church to grow.

Leader: The apostle Paul wrote many epistles to churches he helped start.

Group A: Apostles,

Group B: epistles—

All: words that we should know.

Group A: Some apostles

Group B: wrote epistles,

All: helping the church to grow.

Leader: Other apostles wrote epistles to encourage the church to grow.

Group A: Apostles,

Group B: epistles—

All: words that we should know.

Group A: Some apostles

Group B: wrote epistles,

All: helping the church to grow.

Words of Wisdom

Twenty-one books in the New Testament are letters. Some early Christian leaders wrote these letters to churches and individuals to encourage them to be faithful followers of Jesus.

Look up the verses and fill in the blank lines to discover words of wisdom from the early Christian leaders.

Dear friends, let's _____ each other, because _____ is from God. 1 John 4:7

Now faith, hope, and _____ remain— these three things—and the greatest of these is _____ . 1 Corinthians 13:13

Everyone should be quick to _____ , slow to _____ , and slow to grow _____ . James 1:19

So let's strive for the things that bring _____ and the things that build each other up. Romans 14:19

BONUS: Where do you find a list of people from Bible times who were faithful followers? It sometimes is called the Hall of Faith.

_____

deepbluekids@cokesbury.com

1 Thessalonians 5:16-18

Decorate the verse and the border. Add any other drawings you would like to include. Then cut around the border, and glue your verse to a colored piece of construction paper.

Rejoice always.

Pray continually.

Give thanks in every situation because this is God's will for you in Christ Jesus.

1 Thessalonians 5:16–18

Fruit of the Spirit: Galatians 5:22-23

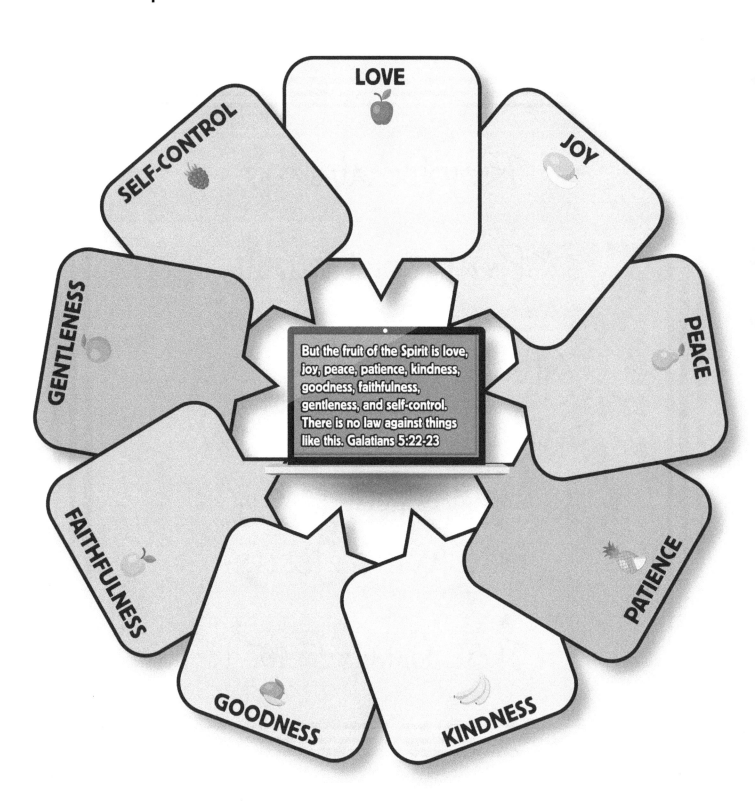

How We Got Our Bible

Use the grid at the bottom to fill in the letters on the blank lines to discover how we got our Bible.

About 3000 B.C., the Egyptians learned to make __ __ __ __ __ __ __ , a __ __ __ __ __ __ -like
1W 1Q 1W 2X 1V 2W 3Z   1W 1Q 1W 2V 1V

material made from reeds. A couple hundred years before Christ, many people began making

__ __ __ __ __ __ __ __ __ from animal skins. Both __ __ __ __ __ __ __ and
1W 1Q 1V 1Z 3Q 2Q 2V 3X 3V   1W 1Q 1W 2X 1V 2W 3Z

__ __ __ __ __ __ __ __ __ were used to make __ __ __ __ __ __ __ . Most of the books of
1W 1Q 1V 1Z 3Q 2Q 2V 3X 3V   3Z 1Z 1V 4Q 2Z 2Z 3Z

the __ __ __ __ __ were first written on __ __ __ __ __ __ __ , and copies of
1X 3W 1X 2Z 2V   3Z 1Z 1V 4Q 2Z 2Z 3Z

these __ __ __ __ __ __ __ were made by hand to use in the synagogues.
3Z 1Z 1V 4Q 2Z 2Z 3Z

Around A.D. 1450, Johannes Gutenberg invented the first printing press.

One of the first books Gutenberg printed was the __ __ __ __ __ .
1X 3W 1X 2Z 2V

	1	2	3	4
Q	A	M	H	O
V	R	E	T	
X	B	Y	N	
W	P	U	I	
Z	C	L	S	

Helps and Tools

Most Bibles that help you dig deeper into God's Word include different symbols. Some of these symbols will help you understand what the Bible says; other symbols will help you explore the Bible more. Are you ready for an adventure through the *CEB Deep Blue Kids Bible*? It's full of symbols to help you.

 Sailboat—notes that help us grow stronger with God by pointing out positive traits we can have in our lives (Example: p. 1377, 1 John 3:18)

 Umbrella—notes that give us help for difficult times by explaining how unhappy emotions and traits aren't good for us (Example: p. 1101, Matthew 25:14-30)

 Lighthouse—notes that help us develop rock solid faith by discussing the basics of following God for life (Example: p. 330, 1 Samuel 16:7-13)

 Life Preserver—notes that give us answers to tough questions and hard-to-understand sections of the Bible (Example: p. 1276, 1 Corinthians 12)

 Did You Know?—call-outs that point out interesting Bible trivia, customs, and practices (Example: p. 1375)

 God's Thoughts / My Thoughts—devotions that help us dive deeper by explaining how the Bible applies to life today (Example: p. 1361, James 3:1-10)

 Navigation Point!—memory verses that mark key promises and passages to memorize (Example: p. 570, Esther 4:14)

Bet You Can!—reading challenges that encourage us to read the Bible for ourselves (Example: p. 1205, John 20:1-18)

BIBLE EXPLORATION TOOLS

Discovery Central—a dictionary that includes more than 350 words with definitions (Example: The dictionary is on pp. 1410–25. Look up the definition of *glory*.)

I Wonder What to Do When I Feel...—verses that point us to promises and actions to take when we don't know what to do (Example: The verse list is on pp. 1426–28. Look at the list, choose a feeling, and then choose a verse to read from that feeling.)

Maps—show the cities and land during Bible times (Example: Map 2 at the back of the Bible. What mountain is located at C5? What happened on that mountain?)

Bible Scavenger Hunt

Look at the Contents pages in your Bible to find the answers. Then write your answers on the blank lines.

1. Find the first book of the Old Testament in the Bible.

   _____

2. Find the first book of the New Testament in the Bible.

   _____

3. Find a book of the Bible that is named for a man.

   _____

4. Find a book of the Bible that is named for a woman.

   _____

5. Find a book of the Bible that begins with the letter Z.

   _____

6. Find a book of the Bible that is in the Prophets division.

   _____

7. Find a book of the Bible that is in the Old Testament History division.

   _____

8. Find the last book of the New Testament.

   _____

9. Find the last book of the Old Testament.

   _____

10. Find a book in the Old Testament with a number in front of its name.

    _____

11. Find a book of the Bible that is in the Gospels.

    _____

12. Find the book of the Bible that tells about the growth of the church.

    _____

13. Find a book of the Bible that is a letter Paul wrote to a church.

    _____

14. Find the book of the Bible that tells about Creation.

    _____

Psalm 119:9-11a Litany

I Keep Your Word Close, in My Heart

How can young people
keep their paths pure?

By guarding them according
to what you've said.

Close in my heart,
close in my heart—
I keep your word close,
in my heart.

I have sought you
with all my heart.

Don't let me stray from
any of your commandments!

Close in my heart,
close in my heart—
I keep your word close,
in my heart.

I know that God's Word
is a beacon of light
along my life's pathway
by day and by night.

Close in my heart,
close in my heart—
I keep your word close,
in my heart.

Adapted from Psalm 119:9-11a.